The Republic of Virtue

THE REPUBLIC OF VIRTUE

Poems by

Paul Lake

The University of Evansville Press
Evansville, Indiana

Printed in the United States of America
First Edition

The text of this book is composed in Baskerville.
Composition by R.G.
Manufacturing by Thomson-Shore.
Book and Cover Design: W.B. & R.G.

Library of Congress Cataloging-in-Publication Data

Lake, Paul, 1951–
[Poems. Selections]
The Republic of Virtue / By Paul Lake. — First Edition.
pages cm
ISBN-13: 978-0-930982-73-7
ISBN-10: 0-930982-73-8
I. Title.
PS3562.A379A6 2013
811'.54—dc23

2013039095

Some of the poems in this collection have been published or are forthcoming in *Alabama Literary Review*, *Arkansas Arts Chronicle*, *Chronicles: A Magazine of American Culture*, *Edge City Review*, *The Evansville Review*, *First Things*, *The Formalist*, *The Hudson Review*, *The Iowa Review*, *Measure: A Review of Formal Poetry*, *Modern Age*, *Pivot*, *Poetry*, *Quadrant*, *Sewanee Review*, *Sparrow*, *Trinacria*, and *Witness*.

The University of Evansville Press
1800 Lincoln Avenue
Evansville, IN 47722
(812) 488-2963

For Tina, Rachel, and Alex

CONTENTS

IV. A Local Habitation and a Name

I. Home Free

First Fruit

First knowledge is the bitterest fruit.
Before it's made more palatable by years,
it sticks in the throat, intractable to reason
and won't be moved by any calculus
of motive or advantage.
                                        It's not my son
discussing death around the kitchen table,
naming who will die
in chronological order down to him
with an actuary's emotionless precision,
but my daughter's first unseasoned cry,
"But is my *Daddy* going to die?"
and how she wracked the house with sobs and wouldn't hear
either rhyme or reason
as she choked on salt, immitigable tears.

Home Free

You storm out late at night
And walk the streets alone
In adolescent pique —
A tried and true technique
To give your folks a fright,
Imagining you half-grown,
A girl not quite fourteen,
Caught in a passing light
On some deserted lane
Or leafy cul-de-sac,
Where danger lurks unseen,
Crouched like a maniac.

At first, I spurn the bait
And watch the clock and phone
With feigned indifference,
Refusing to succumb
To scenes imagination
Plays on its lurid screen,
Till out of patience and
Heart climbing in my throat,
I grab my keys, cell phone,
And hit the empty street
To track your shadow down
Among the leafy shades
And mildly spreading lawns
Of our small Southern town.

At twice the posted speed,
I double back and scan
Each dark unpeopled scene
Still as a Christmas garden,
Where houses sleep, serene
At quarter past eleven . . .
Until, not far ahead,
In pools where shadows spread
Beyond the streetlamps' glow,
I spy a silhouette
And awkward loping gait
That makes my engine slow.

I pull along beside
And start the old debate,
While you walk on, eyes straight,
In unreasoning pride
Refusing to get in,
However much I chide,
Or threaten and cajole.
Then with a quick U-turn,
You duck away and hide
Across a neighbor's lawn
Beyond my headlights' sweep —
Until the truth strikes home —
That you're not mine to keep —
And rounding one last block,
I leave you to the dark
Paths you must tread alone
And slowly circle back
To end our hide-and-seek,
Till love calls us back home
By separate paths, to sleep.

The Ballroom of Heaven

As a Boy Scout, Dad decoded
The *dit-dit-dahs* of Morse, the swashed flags
Of semaphore, bugled "Taps."
At war's end, trumpeted jazz,
Sported a dashing Errol Flynn mustache,
Drove a Mercury coupe, led a brass swing band.

Growing gray, he bought a Mustang,
Captained boats down the Chesapeake,
Tracked game, and bow-hunted bear
In the snow-packed Appalachians.

A snappy salesman with the gift of gab,
He spoke loquaciously, and loved to boast
Of his singular prowess — how he closed a sale,
Bagged a buck, or sang a tenor solo.
Rising late, he rode his route,
Carrying customers' cash, lugged
A black debit book, big as the Baltimore directory
Bound in crocodile hide, holstered a Colt
Semiautomatic, and often flashed
The gold badge bestowed by the Sheriff
When he ran the county's Democrats.

Then cause and effect was suddenly
Suspended. He got lost in a crossword
As in a cul-de-sac. Was flummoxed by phones
As if after Babel. His tongue got
All tangled, his words turned to blab.

Now housed in a hospice, he greets his grown children
"Good guy, good guy," misplacing their names.
Seeing the woman he once swept off the dance floor
And the daughter named after the music they made,
He draws blanks — while a bunch of balloons,
Like a gaggle of gossips who gibber behind him,
Distract his attention, till he's almost unglued.

Pliant as clay, he grows softer and kinder,
More rarefied — as if refined by affliction.
As we quietly mourn his premature absence
And mortified pride, our prayers turn to *Please,*

Let wings take him up now   to the ballroom of heaven
As a brassy young boy   he took up the horn.
Let him trumpet the tunes   that wooed his young wife.
Make melody again.   Dance the jitterbug of joy.

Jogging the Bona Dea Trail

Whether or not we take the longest trail,
Called Serendipity, or simply take
The path to Walden Pond (a man-made lake),
A large map has drawn everything to scale
At the park's entrance: any way we choose —
From paths called Rabbit Run and Prairie Way
To the Swinging Bridge — offers familiar views,
Of pond and field, though what I mean to say
Is that despite the wooden ironies
Of verse I post along the way like signs,
Each foreknown pleasure of my life with you
Is like our jogging: crossing the Dark Slough,
We leave behind the Black Swamp's stricken trees
And walk to light through miles of scented pines.

Thumblings

Far more than Once Upon a Time,
A lonely would-be single-mom
Wished for a child, and one soon came,
Not in the usual way — but sprung
From golden seed of barley corn
Sold by a fairy. And when it bloomed,
A little unborn maiden stood
Among the flower's velvet stems,
So small, a shell served for her bed.

She slept beneath a counterpane
Of rose leaves, till a thieving toad
Abducted the unknowing child
To make her the unwilling bride
Of darkness in an underworld
Of labyrinthine tunnels where
A blind mole made his fetid den.

Or else a couple who bemoaned
Their childlessness conceived a son
Curled like a cashew in the womb,
A shadow pulsing like a drum
No bigger than his father's thumb,
Like pictures on a sonogram,
And in but three months, out came Tom.

Now dressed in cobwebs, thistledown,
And apple rinds, our little Tom

Mourns being traded for the coin
That made his parents prosperous
But him a tiny beggared orphan;
While Thumbelina, like swansdown
Floats in the wind on borrowed wings,
Still haunted by the wedding gown
Woven by spiders her dark groom,
Clad in black velvet, dressed her in.

Now she's escaped that narrow tomb,
Riding a swallow pierced by thorns
Who resurrected from the dead
To fly her to where tulips bloom
And thumblings fill the sky with laughter:
So Thumbelina and Tom Thumb
Have found a happy ever after.

Lullaby

Hush, child, invisible
As thought or silent prayer
Around a supper table,
Restless and fugitive,
Dear ghost, if you are able,
Consider the young pair
Whose adolescent love
Had not grown full enough
To grant you a small share,
And, for love's sake, forgive
Those suffered now to live
In love beneath one roof,
By absence made your heirs.

Herod's Confusion

As her dance dissolves and smiling Salome
Sashays across the floor in smoky veils
To join her scheming mother, Herod sighs,
Seeing how foolishly he's just behaved —
Losing his head to such a vapid girl,
Whose liquid rippling of breasts and thighs
Writhing in time to pipes and throbbing drums
Had teased a promise from him worth a kingdom.

His feet still tapping on the marble floor,
He sees his bride Herodias convey
Her wishes to the girl, then Salome
Mincing across the tiles, at whose request
For John the Baptist's head served on a dish,
A knot of horror tightens in his chest.
He eyes his wife and stepchild with disgust,
Seeing how they, with threads of pride and lust,
Have tied him in a knot he can't escape.
Bound by his word to honor the girl's wish,
He issues orders curtly, to save face
Before his guards and guests . . . and only later,
As rumor of a new redeemer spreads,
Curses the witching music and wild dance
That tricked him from a world of consequence
Into a state where sad-eyed holy men
Whirl past in blurring veils of incarnation.

II. The Republic of Virtue

"The time is out of joint. O cursed spite,
That ever I was born to set it right."

Martyr of Modernity

Christ had his cross. Antoine Lavoisier,
Discoverer of matter's conservation,
When sentenced by the frenzied Paris mob
For crimes against the state, used the occasion
To make a last experiment. To see
How long a brain could live deprived of blood,
He asked a friend to mount the guillotine
And lift his severed head and count his blinks
Before all thought devolved to chemistry,
Then bravely gazed until the last: thirteen.

The Republic of Virtue

In Year One, the month of *Vintage*, time began.
Fog hovered above the earth, like an emanation
Of spirits underground. The scents of rosewater
Sprinkled on sawdust, bird lime, blood and fungus
Commingled in the air, like a chimera
Exhaled from broken mouths. The word *Virtue*
Rumbled above the roar of distant cannon
Like muffled drums, drowning our lamentations.
Nude women promenaded down the streets
As the Marquis de Sade stepped blearily from prison
To raucous cheers. On crumbling balustrades
We fired guns and wept like communicants.

"Man is born free, but is everywhere in chains,"
Declared Rousseau. To break the Social Contract
And signify a city stripped of saints,
The twelve months were reborn, the weeks transfigured
To *decades* of ten days. Without a Sabbath
To toll the bells, a shining new Republic
Of Virtue was proclaimed. De-christened streets
Wore names of heroes. One Easter Sunday morning,
De Sade lured a young beggar named Rose Keller
To his chateau and bound her there in chains,
Enacting scenes he'd first composed in prison
In *Justine, or The Misfortunes of Virtue*,
Till, slipping her restraints, the girl escaped.

"Revolutions, my friend, are not made out of rosewater,"
Cried Danton, as The Committee of Public Safety
Sent spies among the crowd to sniff complaints.
Addressing fellow citizens as "Ladies"
Could lead to steps where other traps were sprung
And heads sent rolling. "If virtue be the spring
Of government in peace," roared Robespierre,
"The spring of government in revolution
Is virtue joined with terror . . . ." In *Thermidor,*
The month of heat, his words rolled to their term
Among piled corpses. Women doused the ground
With rosewater, as choirs of children cheered,
Rags pressed against their mouths to blunt the odor.

For "Terror is only justice, prompt, severe
And inflexible; it is then an emanation
Of virtue . . ." On the streets renamed for saints
Of the Revolution, we celebrate Feast Days
Named *Virtue*, *Genius*, *Labor*, *Payments*, *Reason.*
From *Fog* to *Fruit*, we watch the months revolve
To *Thermidor* again. We watch our tongues
And sniff the air for portents. In strange seasons,
Counting our numbered days. Thinking "If the spring
Of government in peace be virtue," terror
Lurks at the crossroads, smiling, suave, severe.
An aging libertine, extending terms
To beggar girls. Exacting in return
For martyred flesh, the spirit's liberation.
In Declarations born of blood and tears.

Moll

Despite your author's quaint intention
To make a lesson of your life
And show us vice's slow progression
("Twelve year a whore, five times a wife"),
What we retain is the impression
Of how an efficacious creed
Of unrelenting self-possession
Can win the day, the dough, the deed.

For money can ameliorate
The worst disaster, and reverse
Ill fortune, if one's profligate
Of flesh, but stingy with a purse.
A judge's sentence can be bought
Like fish at market, or a nurse
Engaged to rear what was begot
Of cold commercial intercourse.

No sensual delight or passion
Outshines gold coin or silver plate.
Kisses don't keep, but you can cash in
Damask, and pearls are worth their weight.
Friendship's fool's gold; though it might flash in
The eye a moment, it won't keep
A woman housed or dressed in fashion
Like silver in a splendid heap.

O true Madonna of our age,
Your life's a parable that proves
That pensions are sin's only wage,
And that though every bond dissolves
A clever girl can leverage
New deals till time depreciates
Her beauty, then with stolen cache
Purchase herself a fresh estate.

Intolerance: A Memo

Hate those who hate or be among the hated.
The truth grows clearer with each passing day:
Intolerance cannot be tolerated.

Don't think you're safe; no one's inoculated.
Hate means whatever public voices say;
Inflaming first the hater, then the hated,

It spreads whenever ideas are debated
That might cause some discomfort or dismay.
Intolerance cannot be tolerated.

So here's a list of things you've advocated
Now and again which might lead some astray;
Hate them, or find yourself among the hated

Who think intolerance can be abated
By honesty, equality, fair play.
Intolerance cannot be tolerated,

A thought so true, it can't be overstated,
Or brook deliberation or delay.
Hate those who hate or be among the hated.
Intolerance cannot be tolerated.

Epilogue to "The Emperor's New Clothes"

Returning from his proud procession,
The king was pleased by the parade:
His ministers left the impression
That emperors must be obeyed.
Despite some murmurings, the crowd
Ignored the witness of their senses.
Whatever small boys cry aloud,
The truth is woven from consensus.

Those weavers were a subtle pair
Who put folk in a double bind
By claiming if their looms looked bare,
The viewer had a simple mind
Or was unfit for public trust,
And pantomimed cloth into being
So well their dupes learned to adjust
Perception to correct mere seeing.

Based on the way the first could trim
The facts to craft a fabrication,
The emperor appointed him
His Minister of Information.
Now on the nightly news he spins
Transparent fictions into lines
And patterns to clothe royal sins
And cloak imperial designs.

The second weaver scissored air
And mimicked weaving on his frames
So well, he earned a tenured chair
And now employs his language games
To show what lies beneath all texts
Is nothingness, or an illusion.
Revolt's the last thing one expects
Of children tutored in confusion.

Now universally disdained
For spoiling their festivity
The loud-mouthed boy is being trained
To show more sensitivity.
He's learned the first law: *Don't offend.*
Though privately he still might glower,
He's found it's better if you bend
Whenever truth confronts raw power.

Terminals

We wait for something without knowing what.
Bored or distracted, in the screen's fixed glare,
We surf the Net above the deeps of thought.

When no one's looking, we cruise sites for smut,
Downloading tits and twirling pubic hair,
Waiting for something without knowing what,

Or, shutting out the office scuttlebutt,
We play clandestine games of solitaire,
Surfing the Net above the deeps of thought.

We're hardly ever doing what we ought.
There's somewhere else to which our minds repair.
We wait for something without knowing what.

Books gather dust. In information's glut,
We seek excitement somewhere, anywhere,
Surfing the Net above the deeps of thought.

Life is a terminal, a narrow rut.
We long for e-mail like an answered prayer.
We wait for something without knowing what.
We surf the Net above the deeps of thought.

Charlemagne's Vision

Remembering his father's last campaign
To purge the south of Saracen and Moor
And how Grandfather stopped the tide from Spain,
Driving the Muslims from the fields of Tours,
King Charlemagne surveyed the scattered dead
At Roncesvalles, where Roland's ivory horn
Lay shattered on the ground beneath his head,
Then left his slaughtered Paladins, to mourn,

And saw, in troubled sleep, a second Rome
Encoiled by hydra heads — a living net
Encircling London, Paris, Amsterdam,
Each serpent-head poised like a minaret
Above the drowsy heart of Christendom —
Loud cries, bright shafts, red flames, a streaking jet,
Then bodies bowed down in a vast salaam.

Lessons from Gaza

Seized by the spirit of the Lord,
He killed a lion with bare hands,
Slew thirty men without a sword,
And slaughtered foes by the battalion
With just the jawbone of an ass;
Tied firebrands to jackals' tails,
Then loosed them in the enemy's corn,
Burning vineyards, fields, and groves
Until his hair and strength were shorn.
Then captive, broken, chained, and blind,
Encircled by a festive crowd,
He grasped their temple's central posts,
Called on his god and pulled them down,
Killing himself and crushing his hosts
Into the dust of Palestine.

What is the moral of this tale?
What else but that, when building nations,
To nurse a grudge for generations;
To preface slaughter with a prayer;
To jawbone foes when weapons fail;
To stand apart while loosing jackals;
To catch your foes packed into temples
Or market squares and kill wholesale.

A Sleeper

"What do you mean, you sleeper? Arise, call upon your god!"
—Jonah 1:6

A voice said, "Go, and proclaim the destruction of Nineveh,"
And out of the desert I came, like a whirling storm
To humble her pride, to call down fire and brimstone,
To topple her towers and harrow her fertile fields
With salt of tears, to blast her teeming bazaars,
Heralding doom like a dark avenging angel.

I bought my ticket and waited in the narrow cabin
While the passengers tossed on deck and the long ship bucked;
I was eager to die
While the others paled and clutched at their brine-drenched throats,
And was glad when the sea gulped me down
To languish in the fishy entrails of Leviathan time
Till disgorged on your shore, to admonish a godless people.

While hunched in a shabby room in a smoke-clogged lane
East of Nineveh, I surveyed the gray skyline,
Gorging myself on forbidden luxuries,
And eyeing your brazen women
With a hunger born in deserts of deprivation.
I longed to see your livestock staggering, your armored troops
Disarmed, your upright citizens
Appalled by ash and sackcloth,
But in the end,
Found myself railing at God's inhuman mercy
For discharging his bolt in a flicker of summer lightning
In place of a holocaust.

Now a worm gnaws the shading branch above my head
And a hot wind blows from the east
As I drift through this alien city,
Like a wind-borne plague,
Breathing pestilence
Among crowds packed and numberless as cattle.

Revised Standard Version

I'm minding my own business at the well
When up he walks, wagging his prophet's beard
And smiling like he's God's own gift to women.
"Give me a drink," he says as bold as day —
As if I'd nothing better to do there
Than bow beneath his patriarchal whiskers
And fetch him water with a servile grin.
I should have cut him right off at the ankles
Right there and then, but he was young and tall
And seemed so free and easy in his manners,
It put me off my guard.
                                        We talked awhile,
And he seemed nice enough — until he said
Right out of nowhere, "Woman, fetch your husband"
With a sharp look that made me drop my eyes
And stare down at the dust between my feet.

I told him that I didn't have a husband.
"You're right,' he said, "for though you've now had five,
The man with whom you're living isn't one."

I don't know what his game was, but I knew
I wouldn't let him take that tone with me.

"My sex life, sir, is none of your damn business.
I don't know where you got your information,
But if you try this sort of thing again,
I'll haul you into court, you stalker, you.
Who do you think you are, harassing me?"

By now a crowd had gathered at the well curb —
Women with pitchers murmuring approval
And mocking the stranger with loud barbs and sneers.

"Yeah, keep your phony doctrines off my body!"

"I've had a dozen 'husbands' just this year."

"I'll take charge of my sexuality,
With no advice from you, Mr. Misogynist . . ."

He turned back to his friends with a wan look
And left the well to loud catcalls and jeers.
We gathered up our pitchers and assembled
Along the dusty road to Samaria,
Waving our scarves above our heads and singing
Words not set down in your official Greek.

End of the Road

When all roads led to Rome,
unRoman ways
made inroads
into Rome
so Rome's ways changed.
Now when strangers go
to Rome,
to do what Romans do,
neither they
nor Romans know
what Romans do, to do,

some even deeming
it unRoman
they once knew.

III. A Lesson in Hermeneutics

A Lesson in Hermeneutics

In Kenya, vervet monkeys take the ground
Until a sentry gives a chattering bark,
Which in the simple vervet lexicon
Means *snake,* and connotes *evil*, *death*, and *dark.*
Or else the sentry makes a guttural sound
That translates in our own more complex tongue
To *hawk* or *eagle* circling for prey,
And sends the monkeys scampering. Either way,
The monkeys must take action — jump or flee
Across the ground or to a sheltering tree.
Should one, instead, hearing a sentry speak,
Decide to deconstruct the fellow's meaning
And prove all urgent chattering oblique,
A python's fang or hawk's cruel curving beak
Will punctuate the monkey's idle preening,
Ending his dissertation in mid-squeak.

Professing Rape

Come, step into my office. Sit down. Please.
I understand your nervousness in coming
And promise not to step beyond the bounds
You set for conversation. And yet without
Touching on your specific allegations,
I must express my shock and disappointment
At what you're doing and urge you privately
To drop these groundless charges and think how
In instigating such an inquisition
Into our private conduct, you expose
Not only me to forms of discipline
You'd otherwise despise, but open yourself
To charges that you lack a deep commitment
To the theoretical principles you espouse.
As your teacher, then, and one-time counselor,
Let me review our present situation
And urge you toward a different account,
Reminding you that no interpretation
Is ever true or final, since events
Are sealed off from the hermeneutic circle
Of discourse, leaving us to choose between,
Not truth and falsehood, but competing fictions;
And that, however truly you intend
To give a strict and accurate account
Of what transpired between us in recent days,
Your testimony must inevitably
Contain within it subtle gaps and fissures
That crack its logic and disseminate
New meanings in an endless play of signs.

As a student, you were always quick to grasp
Such acid logic and apply it to
Official codes and canons of decorum.
I therefore must conclude this little drama
Is but the latest round in the endless play
Of dominations that has constituted
The ever-shifting web of our relations —
A clever ploy designed to elevate
Your status here and in the discipline,
And not, as you so disingenuously
Aver in this vile letter to the Dean,
A chance to "set the record straight" concerning
My "sexual misconduct . . . harassment . . . rape . . ."
That host of lies and misrepresentations
By which you hope to blacken my good name,
And salve a guilty conscience.

There, you see,
I understand the delicate situation
You find yourself in now — a lover spurned,
A scholar whose best work has been found wanting
And now must justify her flagging efforts
By turning on her friend.
What shocks me more
Than any allegation is the way
You play the martyr so convincingly,
Pretending to an uncritical faith
In words to represent our situation
Objectively, and offering as proof
Of my malfeasance such ambiguous signs
As soiled clothes and vaguely worded letters —
As if you had forgotten it was I

Who trained you in interpretative methods,
Or thought that, having taught you to expose
The circular interplay of power-knowledge
That animates all discourse, I'd abandon
Rank and authority to play the villain
In this, your sordid feminist melodrama.

Let me remind you then what years of study
Have failed to teach: That you are nothing more
Than a de-centered and fragmented subject,
A point or node within a fluid skein
Of many texts and contexts, the product of
Immense impersonal technologies
Of control — powerless, insignificant —
And not a sovereign "self" that I've "debased."
What pains me most in this grotesque affair
Is how you've spurned such hard-won, painful knowledge
To play the innocent, forgetting how
Language, like your languid female body,
Can by its very slipperiness betray
Unauthorized desires, exposing itself
To fresh interpretation.
                                        The seminal
Stains you pose as evidence of rape
Might just as well support a different case;
The faint half-hearted protests and denials
You offered might seem tokens of defense
Designed to pacify the speaker's conscience
Or silence memories of how you came
Alone that night to visit my apartment,
And, drinking freely, later woke to find
Your flesh become the happy medium

Of unspeakable sensations, exquisite torments
Of understanding . . . agonized assents . . .
Till even your post-coital sobs and sniffles
Incited lust to more transgressive passions . . .

But that's all past. I see your face is set
In a grim mask of humorless resistance.
You'll play your scene and have your little say.
But be assured, if you subject my person
To official probes and formalized procedures,
I'll paint you as a clever scheming slut
Promiscuous in language as in morals;
I'll characterize your words as perjury
And brand your scholarship as plagiarism.
And since there's no authoritative version
Of past events with which to square accounts,
You'll sacrifice your chances of employment
For the dubious solace of a failed revenge.
Because, my dear, in cases such as this
Where lines are drawn and facts are fluid texts,
It all comes down to your word against mine.

Allegory of the Bees

Affectless drones, observing the wild dance
Of honey-drudgers, smile with condescension
At the ecstatic mass's naive notion
That waggled steps can measure a straight course
To hidden nectar, or unplotted land
Be spanned and mapped by buzzing blurring signs,
While honey-drudgers leave in steady lines,
Tracking the legend to its honeyed source.

The Tower of Babel

When words were few and men spoke with one tongue,
We joined together with a common aim:
To make a ziggurat so straight and strong
It touched the sky and scored it with our name.
And so, bound to one purpose, we began
Moving in concert, with a single voice
Vociferously approving our great plan,
And mounted heavenward by common choice.

Then loudly (over muttered cries of *treason*)
A mason said it lacked a cornerstone
Of universal truth and human reason
To ground it firmly, and that each alone
Was laboring futilely unplugging drains
To keep a pile of melting sun-baked bricks
From slumping in a wash of summer rains;
That common bonds were chains; that politics
And universal happiness disguised
A system by which evil patriarchs
Enslaved our thoughts, he further theorized,
Stamping our own clay with our master's marks.

Then in the hush, a scribe was overheard
To say that words themselves were prone to slide
Like muddy bricks, till definitions blurred
And none could tell what things they signified.

Once every builder came to understand
Our lovely language was a set of tricks,

Our tongue and tower built on shifting sand,
And we shaped, stamped, and laid in rows like bricks,
We railed against the evil Will-to-Power
That gulled us with the sinister illusion
That we could make a name or build a tower,
And, laying down our tools, fell to confusion
And scattered through the earth with little sense
Of purpose till those similarly inclined
Discovered cultures in their difference
And learned to speak with one voice and one mind.

Echoes

A dolphin, like a bat or sonar dish,
Turns sonic blips to solid information
Till, bored with his one-sided conversation
With ocean floors and passing schools of fish,
He turns to higher forms of mimicry
And imitates his own returning wave
With cunningly cast measures that behave
To dolphin ears like carvings by Bernini,
Transforming shoal and branching coral reef
To frozen arias of sculpted sound
So artfully that others might confound
Its delicately etched patterns in relief
With star or angelfish, or, hearing, feel
The shock of truth like an electric eel.

A Language Game

All words are null and void, a language game
We circle round like children in a ring,
Singing ring-around-the-rosy, skeptics claim.

Try summoning a rose by its red name
To breathe its scent: you'll feel the sudden sting
Of counters voided in a language game

Like cancelled checks. Or shuttled on a frame
Where crimson thought won't stitch to one read thing.
It's ring-around-the-rosy, skeptics claim.

Yet flouting such sound logic, poets aim
To seize the brazen truth like a brass ring,
Spinning their counters in the language game

To arias and orchids, flash and flame,
To lullabies, and seraphim who sing
Of *ring* and *rose* and *posies,* till none claim

To tell the who or what from what they name
And only skeptics, trapped in sentencing,
Are null and void. Though but a language game,
Sing *ring-around-the-rosy* just the same.

IV. A Local Habitation and a Name

Testament

In this, my fortieth year of age,
I wake beneath a soggy sheet
Stone sober, my mind a crumpled page,
My life a sentence, half complete;
Still mired in the old conceit
And lust for literary fame,
I stare down darkness, death, defeat,
Burning my candle in the game.

I think of Baudelaire's refrain —
"Get drunk! — on wine or poetry,
On virtue, hashish, crack cocaine —
But get drunk ceaselessly, or be
In moments of sobriety
Another martyred slave of time" —
And how, on such authority,
For twenty years, I've binged on rhyme.

But now, in more prosaic days,
I see my life's been chiefly spent
(While others won the jobs, the bays)
In silence, exile, unemployment,
And third-rate posts; my sole enjoyment,
Arranging words in borrowed rooms,
For which, to meet demands for rent,
I've sold possessions, hocked heirlooms —

In short, behaved like any addict
Who mortgaged future time to buy

(Instead of houses) one more crack
At fame, that last infirmity
Of feeble minds. I bet on poetry,
That swaybacked Pegasus, whose wings
Have been clipped by modernity
To Hallmark cards and "Elvis Sings!"

Ah God, had I instead pursued,
With such ambition, more degrees
Or shown a higher aptitude
For essaying in Theorese —
"Engendering the Boundaries
Of Discourse: Gay's Transgressive Plays,"
Or "(De)Constructing Patriarchy's
Cruel, Objectifying Gaze" —

I'd teach at Yale — or Kansas State;
I'd spend my summers in Milan;
I'd edit, collate, annotate,
And publish work in *Raritan*.
I'd have a house, a minivan,
A Macintosh, and two grants pending.
Returning from the Caribbean,
I'd vow to cut back on my spending.

Too late for that. At forty, who
Can overthrow a lifetime's vices?
I'll spend my life in Timbuktu
Composing verse, although the price is
A bleak old age, enduring crisis,
And thoughts embittered by the knowledge
That cash alone is what suffices.
A name won't put my kids through college.

And so, like Crusoe on his isle,
I put the State of my Affairs
In writing — not as in a Will,
Since I am like to have few Heirs —
But setting Comforts against Cares,
And weighing Bad against the Good,
As Debtors do with Creditors,
To soothe myself as best I could:

I am cast up in Russellville,
Void of all hope of Rescue. Good:
But could be teaching in Brazil
Or in a crime-filled neighborhood.
I'm separated from the World
Of Letters, banished from humane
Society; alone; exiled.
But have the mail, stamps, and a phone.

I have few Clothes to cover me.
True, but nowhere else to go.
No talk — but book clubs wonderfully
Supply the occasional *bon mot.*
And so on . . . till, upon the whole,
I'm reconciled to my condition
As well, almost, as R. Crusoe —
Except my life is not a fiction.

What use to moan and beat my breast,
Curse fate, or slander my vocation,
Counting myself among the oppressed
Because I've reached no higher station.
I give a local habitation
To airy nothing, and a name

To shapes formed in imagination,
Burning my candle in the game.

Carpe Diem

Over plain and plateau, you go, long tongue lolling,
As far up ahead on the Arizona sand,
Your feather-brained nemesis is rapidly roaring
Over gulch, flat, and arroyo in a blue blur of smoke.

O Wile E. Coyote, won't you ever wise up
To the truth, that that blue bird's an unlikely catch?
All your tar pits and glue traps, your *trompe l'oeil* painted billboards
Only catch or confound you, while Road Runner flees.
Your dynamite delays, fuses fizzling like sparklers
Till your prey's out of range, then explodes in your face.

Still, you strap on Icarian wings, an Acme rocket,
And, confidently posing yourself on the brink
Of another disaster, hear that haunting *meep-meep*
That fires up your rockets and sends you flying furiously
Smack into a cliff face . . .
                                        or with featherless wings
For a few frantic seconds treading measureless air,
Till a quick double-take shows your depthless dumb folly
And you curse the first dimwit who said, "Seize the day."

California Condor

He flies almost as near to heaven
as a 747,
yet tangles like a kite in power lines

and camped beneath the dark cloud of extinction,
dreams of his former splendor
in the long-gone Pleistocene,

aware that his beleaguered kind
does not, like the great auk,
lack wings for flight,

nor intellect
like dodos, nor is it clumped
in scrumptious flocks

like the short-lived passenger pigeon.
And yet, in desert gloom,
feeling extinction loom,

he thinks how cruel and unfair
it is to claim a little niche
in thinning air,

to make a nest
of dead dry sticks
on barren rocks,

to dine on carrion
instead of steak,
to own but one

extravagance — a giddy head
for poetry and dizzy heights —
and know such glory wasn't bred

for unsuccess,
but joy, pure joy
that makes his pallid face flush red,

his long curved throat
without a voice box, cry
its tragic note

to sea and sky
while in the tumult down below
his sun-baked perch

a gray torpedo
with gaping maw
and lidless eye

pierces the surf,
unfeeling of its soft caress,
like all his kind

raking a profit from the tide,
a cold heart beating in his chest,
with one thought circling in his head:

success success success success.

Underdog and Overlord

The Underdog
is born to serve
the purpose of
the Overlord,

who serves in turn
the general good
by giving work
to Underdog —

a dogma that
each dog must learn,
according to
the Sacred Word

recorded by
the Overlord,
who with his sword
and pen assured

his lordship
in the human herd.
Until the light
of reason shone

and Underdog
went underground
to post a new word
of his own.

Proclaiming each dog
has his day,
he found that weblog
and broadside

can't underdog-
by-underdog
reshape the world
to suit his need —

not when like broadswords
broadcasts sweep
across the airwaves
in his sleep.

Aspiring now
to greater heights,
the Underdog
worked overtime

and took a college
course by night —
until he heard
his teacher say

that in this dog-
eat-dog world, he
was Underdog,
and, conversely,

that Underdog
was Overlord,

who ruled the whole world
with his sword,

who crushed the weak,
who starved the poor,
whose captains loosed
the dogs of war,

and who for all
of dogdom's good
must have his too-broad
powers curbed.

Astounded at
what he had heard,
the hangdog heart
of Underdog

caught in his throat
till he espied
beneath his tenured
teacher's beard

the flashing teeth
and shining eyes
of Overlord
in a new guise.

Pro Forma

Certain poets, whose measures don't seem to conform
To any known pattern, when pressed will explain,
They're not tin-eared bards when they veer from the norm;
If their meters don't scan and their rhymes crack and strain,
It's not that the rhyme scheme's too hard to maintain —
When their sonnet falls short a few lines, their refrain
Is to sing out in chorus, "The rules don't obtain!
I'm a clever young artist subverting the form!"

Likewise, when a contractor building a dorm
Fails to bolt metal crossbeams or hammer in nails
And the floors start to buckle like ships in a storm
Then collapse, crushing hundreds, though agonized wails
Might suggest that the devil was in the details,
Don't insist that the culprits be thrown into jails,
Show that *you* at least know what good building entails
For a clever young artist subverting the form.

So the next time you're out and the air is aswarm
With pestiferous flies, and the staff smell like minks,
And your coffee's served cold and your sherbet's served warm,
And there's spit on your entrees and piss in your drinks,
Don't storm out in a huff, shouting how the joint stinks,
But instead flash the host, cooks, and servers sly winks —
Let them know you're a modern food critic who thinks
They're all clever young artists subverting the form.

Song of the Living

Not the amniotic fluid where I floated like a fish
While I waited for my mother to give birth,
Not the semi-strangulation of a lank umbilicus,
Not the anaconda coils I traversed,

Not the icky liquids leaking out of every orifice,

I didn't sign up for this.
I didn't sign up for this —

For tapeworms, eye mites, ticks, mosquitoes
Snugly burrowed in,

For eczema, psoriasis,
Or the heartbreak of gangrene,

For blisters, moles, or melanoma's
Slow metastasis —

I didn't sign up for this.
I didn't sign up for this.

If asked, I might have answered that
I wouldn't really care to
Be subject to the thousand shocks
Our mortal flesh is heir to:

The menopause, mastectomy, bone loss and hunching back,
The fibroids, stillbirths, bleeding like a hemophiliac,
The balding, diabetes, impotence, paralysis —

You'll look in vain to find my name inscribed on some contract.

As you too face the same disgraceful metamorphosis,
With night sweats, staring snow-blind into time's breathless abyss,
With bedsores oozing, cold, and diapers full and damp with piss,

At the end of the day
You too will say,
I didn't sign up for this.

In the final analysis
I didn't sign up for this.

Not Gonna Die

"Your Grandpa just got tired," my young mother said to me,
"So we laid him in the ground so he can rest eternally."
Well, I decided then and there, "That plan ain't gonna fly.
I won't never get *that* tired. I am not gonna die."

I might wander in the desert without water for some weeks,
Or lie buried in an avalanche with icicles for cheeks,
I might lose a couple fingers, and my throat might get real dry,
I might *look* a little tired, but I sure ain't gonna die.

If I happen to fall overboard into the stormy sea,
Then I'll do the doggie paddle till I get to Italy.
When my arms and legs grow heavy, I'll switch to the butterfly.
I might seem a little tuckered, but I'm not about to die.

If I'm flying up the off-ramp that I should be going down
And slam into a Mack truck, scattering parts through half the town,
With my teeth stuck in the dashboard and my liver on the fly,
I might look a little poorly, but I'm sure not gonna die.

When I'm wrinkled, deaf and hunchbacked at a hundred forty-three,
I might drowse a bit, but I ain't gonna rest eternally.
When the Reaper comes, I'll smile and fix him with my one good eye
And say, "Friend, don't get your hopes up. I ain't *never* gonna die."

Plumber's Song

"No matter what your time or place is
The hero with a thousand faces
Enacts your fate from the world's storehouse of great myths."
So, Joseph Campbell, please explain
Why I'm now snaking out a drain
To free the sewage of the Johnsons and the Smiths.

Though every sage of the Greek nation
Said a life of contemplation
Is the path to virtue, truth, and happiness,
In my present situation
But for two weeks' paid vacation,
What's to contemplate but daily crappiness?

Flipping burgers, digging ditches
Would teach all those sons of bitches
Who proclaim we should be following our bliss
That life's an open septic tank
We teeter over on a plank
And our sole quest's to keep from plunging into piss.

The Man Who Knew Why Stars Shine

> *"One of the most impressive discoveries was the origin of the energy of stars, that makes them continue to burn. One of the men who discovered this was out with his girlfriend the night after he realized that nuclear reactions must be going on in the stars in order to make them shine. She said 'Look at how pretty the stars shine!' He said, 'Yes, and right now I am the only man in the world who knows why stars shine.' She merely laughed at him."*
>
> — Richard Feynman, *Six Easy Pieces*

He knew why stars shine
But still hadn't learned
That a girl, growing tired
And bored, never yearned
To hear the one man
Who knew why explain
How the stars shine so prettily
Without commenting on
Those stellar attractions
Much closer at hand.
And so with face fired
By internal reactions
He watched as the one
Girl he deeply desired
First laughed at his gravity
Then left him to burn.

A Worm

Held in suspended animation
As in a tale by Arthur Clarke,
We whirl beyond the final station
Into the interstellar dark,

Trusting our software to maintain
Our course through boundless tracks of night
Then warm and wake each dormant brain
Into otherworldly light.

Or else we'll speed through hyperspace
On theme-park ships with tropic air.
However humans interface
Or merge our software with wetware,

Some hidden glitch coiled in our code
Will spread subversion like a worm
And crashing systems for a joke
Bring our odyssey to its term.

Narcissus Reflects

I stare into the pool. Across the lake,
The nymph repeats my final, parting cry —
          "I'd rather die!" —
And weeps to think how for her vengeance's sake
The goddess Nemesis, or Aphrodite,
Condemned me to reflect on my mistake
By staring at this mirror, eye to eye
          With mortal beauty

Until I saw why, stepping into view,
That dumb nymph Echo shook with hope and fear
          As I drew near
And cried so desperately, "I yield to you!" —
As if the mimicry of senseless stone
Was what, among those cliffs, I sought to hear
And not a dialogue, a *pas de deux*
          With the unknown.

Yet, slowly, what began as punishment
Became a blessing. Staring past my face,
          I've learned to trace
In foam-fringed depth and starry firmament,
In cloud and frost, ear's whorl and crystal eye,
Pattern reflecting pattern, until space
Contracts and in a blue bewilderment
          Of pond and sky

I see how in disequilibrium
Chaotic order hovers in suspense
        Till turbulence
Erupts in whirlwind, flower, painted plume,
And ramifying limb, at every scale,
Till, gathered in one magnifying lens,
Imagoes, ranged like seraphim, become
        A coronal,

A budding youth, a poet's branching tale.

The Water Glass

In Memory of Michael Donaghy

When water poised above the rim,
He noted it was surface tension
That held the audience and him
Spellbound. That night, the whole convention
Trembled on edge till Michael quipped,
"What could a surface be tense about?"
And laughter broke like water. Then
He made a splash when he passed out.
The doctors looking at his chart
Were puzzled by the tinny tunes
His organs made, but Michael felt
"A gypsy wedding in my heart,"
And we all laughed. Now it's as if
With flute and whistle, he's danced off
To join that gypsy caravan
In noisy mirth, as dark drips down
Night's tent, beyond the edge of town.

The Author

After graduating from Towson University, Paul Lake was a Stegner Fellow at Stanford, where he received his M.A. He has taught English and Creative Writing at Santa Clara University and Arkansas Tech. Since 2006, he has been the poetry editor of *First Things*. His poems and essays have been widely published, and he has authored two previous poetry collections, *Another Kind of Travel* and *Walking Backward*, as well as two novels, *Among the Immortals* and *Cry Wolf: A Political Fable*.